Bevy's Promise

BEVY'S PROMISE

Phyllis Chunn

Bevy's Promise

Copyright © 2024 by Phyllis Chunn
Text and Illustrations
(Registration# TXu 2-431-275)

All rights reserved.
ISBN: 9798324853792

This book may not be reprinted in full or in part without written permission from the author.

To Punkin.

Forever true!

From a sapling to a grand old tree,

You have stood firmly and rooted in,

Your love and support for me!

                    Thank you, Ma

Contents

Meet Bevy 1

The Four Amigos 8

Fresh Cut Day 12

Bevy's Promise 20

Puddin Pie 35

The Great Revival 52

Birthday Party 58

The Final Tests 64

Test to Testimony 68

Acknowledgements

First and foremost, I must acknowledge my mother, Mary Lee Chunn. I would not be who I am today if not for her prayers and guidance. She is the epitome of the virtuous woman that's referred to in the Bible.

To my children, Carmen Punkin Moore and Michael Chari Baldwin. I am able to keep moving forward because of you both. You are my biggest supporters. I do what I do because of your encouragement and love. Thank you dearly.

To Greg Chunn, my brother from another mother. You saw something in me that I had not realized; and you gave me the nudge to try and believe in the gift God had given me.

Meet Bevy

"Hi, I'm Beverly Ann Thornton, and I am 8 years old. Everyone calls me Bevy except my dad. He calls me his June Bug since my birthday is in June. My birthday was yesterday," Bevy introduced herself to a young girl in the reception area of the Children's Hospital.

The young girl was in a wheelchair, and she was handing out welcome flyers to the new patients.

"I'm Clara, and I am 12 years old, and I live here," Clara extended her hand to greet Bevy, then gave Bevy a welcome pamphlet, smiled and said, "Welcome to Children's Hospital".

Two years ago, Bevy also lived at Children's Hospital. It all started in the middle of the school year. Bevy was in first grade. She began having pain in the left side of her tummy. The pain kept getting worse and she began losing her appetite.

She didn't even want to eat Grammy's flapjacks. Grammy, Mom and Dad knew something was wrong, because Bevy always wanted to eat Grammy's flapjacks drizzled in butter and syrup. So, they quickly took her to see Dr. Helford. Dr. Helford sent them to a new doctor for more tests.

The new doctor is Dr. Michael Chari. His office is at Children's Hospital. Bevy was instantly smitten with Dr. Chari's handsome smile and kind nature. He is admired by all the kids and their parents, and especially the nurses.

After lots of tests and office visits, Bevy and Mom moved to the hospital.

"I don't want to stay here" Bevy cried to her Dad. Through sobs and tears, she tried to listen to her parents reassuring her that they would be with her, and everything was going to be all right. Bevy was only six years old when this happened. She didn't understand why she had to leave home and leave her friends.

It was also puzzling for Bevy to see so many children with no hair, and many kids had little plastic tubes in their noses.

A few days after moving into her room at the hospital, Bevy got her own oxygen tube in her nose. She realized it wasn't so bad.

Each day the nurses were just as excited to see Grammy as Bevy because Grammy always had fresh baked goodies for them.

But the real highlight of Bevy's Day was each afternoon when Dad came from work. She anxiously waited and listened for his footsteps at her door.

Bevy adored her dad. He made her feel safe and could encourage her to smile when no one else could. When he sang, Bevy's spirit would swell with pride.

Dad is a wonderful singer and pianist. Some of Bevy's proudest memories were at church when Dad sang and played the piano for the choir. Whenever anyone complimented him on his singing, he would smile and say, "music soothes the soul."

The Four Amigos

Annette, Shirley, and Barbara Prye were Bevy's best friends from school. Mom called the girls the four amigos because they are inseparable. They did everything together including dressing alike.

The girls send Bevy get-well-soon cards and paper dolls to play with. Dad and the youth choir even made a video of them singing a get-well-soon song for her.

Bevy stayed in Children's Hospital for weeks, and eventually the hospital began to feel like a second home. She made new friends, and everyday there were all types of entertainment, singing, clowns and delicious treats. The positive attitudes of the nurses and other children helped Bevy bare the pricks, prodding and scans she would have to endure each day.

"Read to me Mommy," Bevy would whisper to her mom. Even when Bevy was too weak to open her eyes, and it appeared Bevy was sleeping, Mom would softly read Bevy's favorite bible stories to her. Bevy has always enjoyed her bible stories, but now they seem more important to her because the bible stories relax her. While listening to the stories, her mind would drift away to a beautiful, restful place that has no hospitals and no pain. Pain is something little Bevy knows too well.

No matter how tough things got, she knew in her heart one day she would leave the hospital and return home to her friends and her special tree.

Fresh Cut Day and Feebie

The day came when Bevy was going to the hair salon to get a haircut like the other kids. Mom and Bevy went down to the salon. Grammy hadn't come to the hospital yet.

After her haircut, Bevy chose to wear a headband with a pink rose and sparkles around the band. Mom and Bevy stopped by the smoothie bar to get a berry smoothie before returning to her room. The haircut and the walk through the hallways were exhausting for little Bevy. Once Mom tucked Bevy in bed, she fell asleep before the nurse could finish connecting her monitor and checking her vitals.

Shortly after Bevy awoke from her nap, Grammy walked into the room. "Wow! Look at Grammy" Bevy said. Grammy had the same haircut as Bevy. Grammy had cut her long, beautiful hair to match Bevy's fresh style. Mom and Bevy looked at Grammy with wide-open mouths.

Grammy and Feebie

14

Grammy was smiling and posing in the middle of the floor like a model. Then she walked over to the bed and said, "hey good lookin, what's cookin!" We all laughed and hugged each other tightly.

When we finally stopped laughing, Grammy said, "look darling this is Feebie."

Feebie is a large, red-headed doll with a short haircut like Grammy and Bevy. Feebie became Bevy's favorite sleeping partner.

"She's just the right size and she smells like Grammy's apron," Bevy said as she

rested her head on the doll and drifted off to sleep for her afternoon nap.

As she slept, she dreamed of being at her tree, with her friends singing in the Sunday choir. They were singing, **"He's Got the Whole World in His Hands**." She wore her favorite black choir robe, as she directed the choir.

The robe is actually one of Dad's old black tee shirts that was so big on Bevy's little body, it looked like a long flowing choir robe.

The girls sang loud and proud; everyone was on key for the first time! Annette was even paying attention to her part of the song. She's supposed to sing the chorus, "In His Hands," in her beautiful soprano voice, after each phrase.

Annette came in right on cue which surprised the other girls because she is usually fidgeting and talking, and she always missed her part.

Shirley never missed her part. She held her head back, closed her eyes and blasted out everybody's parts of the song. Shirley loved to sing, and she liked being seen even more.

Barbara Prye's voice was so soft and pretty, she filled in the harmony perfectly.

Bevy directed the choir with perfection. They sang like angels.

Everyone in the church applauded and shouted "Hallelujah, Bravo girls!"

The dream drifted away as Bevy was awakened by a nurse checking her vitals again.

Bevy's Promise

This morning, Bevy was surprised to see Dad at the hospital in the morning instead of at work.

Uh oh, Dad, Mom, Grammy, and Dr. Chari had that serious look on their faces. Bevy was sure they had been talking about something secret.

Grammy would smile at her and say things like, "Bevy is such a brave little girl, and we know everything is going to be just fine."

Dad leaned over, held Bevy's hand, and explained that she was going to have 'a procedure'.

"You don't have to worry because we're here with you June Bug, and you know the Lord has us all in his hands," Dad said reassuringly to Bevy.

"Okay Daddy" Bevy responded. She didn't know what 'a procedure' meant, but she trusted her Daddy.

Later that day Dr. Chari came into her room to get her ready for 'the procedure.'

He said, "It's time little one". Then Dr. Chari gave Bevy medicine to relax her. She went into a deep peaceful sleep.

Bevy was taken to surgery and after surgery, she went to the recovery area. Mom and Grammy sat quietly and watched her sleep the entire time.

Suddenly, Bevy's little hand raised high in the air. She was trying to point upward. The nurse gently guided her hand down to the bed and Bevy smiled as she dreamed.

"Jesus took hold of her hand and told Bevy to wake up. When she opened her eyes, Bevy and Jesus went walking in a beautiful garden of wildflowers. The flowers were dancing back and forth in the breeze and the air smelled like lilac and honeysuckle all mixed together. They walked along a path and found a river with a sparkling waterfall that turned different colors. All around the river and all over the garden were the most beautiful flowers. Some of the flowers were even bigger than the ones in Grammy's Garden.

As she looked around the garden, she could see little furry animals running  around and chasing each other all through the flowers. There were the most beautiful birds singing and fluttering all through the trees.

Jesus and Bevy sat next to the river with their feet dangling in the cool water. The river was full of colorful fish with fancy designs. The fish nibbled at Bevy's toes and made her toes tickle.

It was this moment Bevy knew, everybody was right, Jesus does love us!

She looked around at the amazing sites then asked Him, "Is this Heaven?" Jesus laughed and put his arms around her and said, "No, this is your garden. Don't you remember? There's your castle with the purple unicorns," He pointed to a castle way in the distance. There were two unicorns standing at the castle gate. They looked like Jasper, Bevy's plushy unicorn.

"Is it time for me to go to heaven? I'm not ready to go to heaven yet because I have to take care of my mommy and daddy," Bevy said with concern in her voice. Jesus hugged her tighter and said, "I promise, you will have lived many days, and you will have accomplished many wonderous things before you go to your castle in Heaven."

She awakened to the beeping sound of her monitor and squeezing and releasing of the BP cuff around her arm. There was a terrible pain in her stomach. The doctor wanted her to stay quiet and gave her more medicine so she could sleep longer.

Bevy tried her hardest to stay awake. She wanted to tell everyone about the garden and Jesus.

The next day, Mom attempted to feed Bevy breakfast. Bevy was too excited and she kept trying to tell them about her dream.

"You have to calm down Beverly Ann," Mom said with a serious tone. "You can tell us after you eat something."

"Okay," Bevy said, and she tried to eat the tasteless dish.

After breakfast, Dad said "tell us your dream June Bug."

Bevy blurted out, "Jesus was here!

"Yes honey, Jesus is with us all the time," Mom said.

"No Mom, He was here in this room, and He took me to a beautiful garden. You didn't see Him because you were asleep."

They all thought her garden was just a dream which aggravated Bevy. The nurse gave Bevy more medicine so she could stay calm and rest.

This time as she dreamed, the garden had a different fragrance.

It smelled like the perfume counter at the mall. Bevy ran and played with the furry animals on the soft grass and picked the flowers.

She couldn't see Jesus, but she could feel his presence, she knew he was there.

Each time Bevy woke up, she tried to tell everyone about Jesus and the wonderful garden, but she just couldn't stay awake.

Finally, one morning, Mommy was feeding Bevy breakfast. It was terrible but she tried to eat a few bites to make Mom happy. Bevy tried again telling Mom about Jesus and the garden. Mom told her to calm down and said, "You were just dreaming honey." Grammy winked her eye at Bevy and said, "It's okay darling, we know all about it."

But they didn't know! "I was not dreaming! It is true. Jesus took me to a beautiful garden and made me a promise. He is real, my garden is real," Bevy whispered over and over until she drifted off to sleep.

Late one night while the hospital was quiet, Bevy was lying in bed watching Mom sleeping on the pull-out sofa. Mom slept there every night and refused to go home even when Dad and Grammy insisted.

"My Mom is so pretty and sweet." Bevy thought to herself. Bevy quietly said her prayers and asked Jesus to protect her Mommy and Daddy and Grammy.

At home Bevy would often lay awake at night and enjoy the quiet sounds in their home. During those times, she would have the warmest feelings of love thinking about her parents, Jesus, and her friends.

Before drifting off to sleep, she would listen quietly for the train sounds far away in the night. The sound of the train was relaxing for Bevy. She imagined it going and coming from all sorts of mysterious places.

Puddin Pie

As Bevy snuggled into her covers and started to close her eyes, she saw a little girl peeking in her doorway. Bevy raised her head and smiled at the little girl. The girl pushed the door open, walked in and said in a loud shrill voice, "Hey, I'm Puddin Pie! Bevy put her finger to her mouth, "shhhh, Mommy's sleeping."

"Are you gonna be my best friend?" Puddin Pie asked with a wide smile and missing front teeth.

"I, I guess so" Bevy stammered being a little confused because she had not seen Puddin Pie at the hospital before.

"Okay then, I'll see you laaydeer!" The little girl attempted to sing in a lower voice and walked quickly out the door with that big toothless smile.

Mom looked up from the sofa and said "Bevy, you okay? Do you need something Baby?"

"No ma'am, I'm okay," she answered softly and wondered about the strange little girl.

A few weeks after her surgery, Bevy was able to go home. The nurses gave her a big going home party. There was the traditional bell-ringing ceremony, snacks, and photos with everyone.

She was going to miss seeing Dr. Chari and her new friends, but she was quite excited to go home again.

Nurse Dent will make home visits each week to administer Bevy's medicine for a while.

Bevy's friends are not allowed to visit yet. Dr. Chari says her immune system needs to be a little stronger before she is allowed to have visitors.

At first, Bevy's medicine left her sleepy and weak, but each day Bevy got stronger. Grammy and Bevy walked around outside to get fresh air and sunshine.

Eventually, Bevy began to walk around the yard on her own, and she started spending more time reading at her favorite tree.

You will never believe it! One morning when Bevy was reading in her bedroom, that little girl from the hospital was standing at her doorway flashing a great big smile.

"What cha reading?" she asked with that peculiar little voice.

"A bible story about David and Goliath" Bevy said looking at her with a surprised expression.

"Don't you want some company," she smiled sheepishly.

"Yeah," Bevy answered.

"Well let's go do something fun!" Puddin Pie said while bouncing up and down on Bevy's bed.

"Okay come and go with me. I'll show you my magic tree", Bevy said.

Bevy was excited to have someone to play and talk to besides Grammy. The girls ran through the yard pass Bevy's old swing set until they reached the tree at the rear of the yard.

Underneath the tree was a small table and chair set with dolls and other plushy animals waiting to be served tea and cookies.

"What do you do here," Puddin Pie *asked Bevy?*

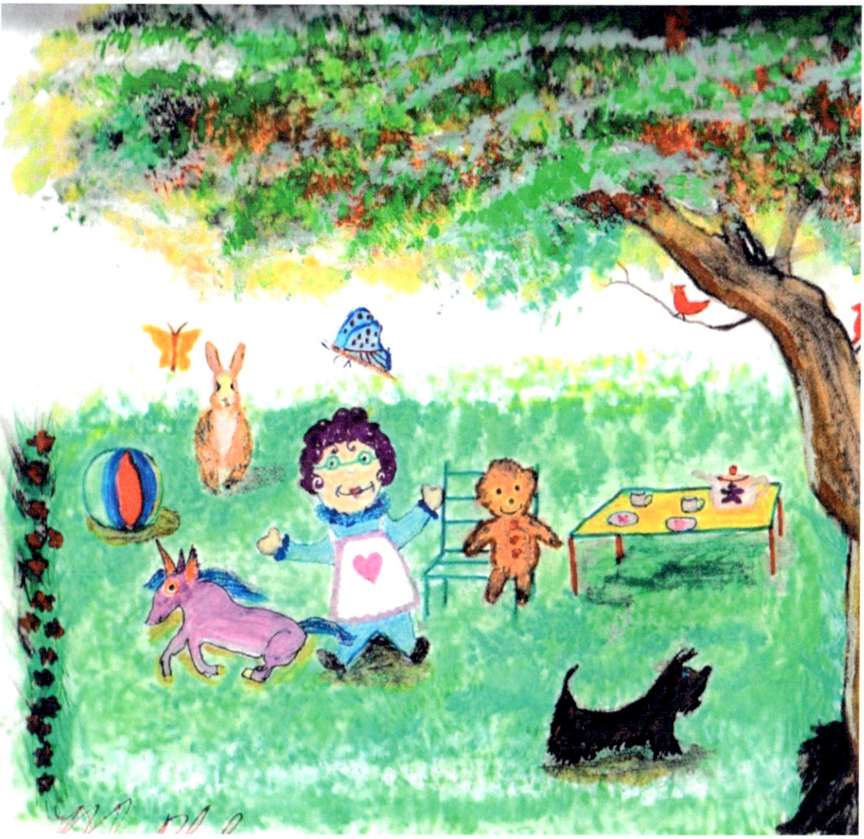

Bevy answered, "Sometimes my friends come over and we play church. We rehearse our choir songs. I'm the choir director. Shirley leads the prayer; she gets down on one knee and pretends to pray like Deacon Burrs. Annette and Barbara take turns shouting and fanning each other like Aunt Effie and Miss Mary," Bevy laughed as she explained all this to Puddin Pie.

"They are my best friends and I miss seeing them, but Mom said they can't come over now because my immune system is too weak."

"Sometimes we play dress up and have tea parties. Let's get up in the tree and find Mrs. Rabbit and the baby bunnies," Bevy said and quickly climbed up into the tree.

Bevy made herself comfortable against a branch. She closed her eyes and said, "Sometimes I just float away to my beautiful castle. My castle is gold and purple and is guarded by unicorns just like Jasper." She pointed to her unicorn plushy that was sitting under the tree.

"I'm so glad you came to visit me Puddin, I get lonely without my friends, I hope you can meet my other friends soon.

They are all in school now," Bevy's voice was a little sad because she missed going to school and being with her friends.

"Look! There's Mrs. Rabbit and the babies!" She jumped down from the tree to sneak up to the rabbits, but they quickly scurried away.

MRS. RABBIT

"Be careful June Bug," she heard dad say from the patio. He was sitting there reading a newspaper while mom was inside preparing dinner.

Mrs. Rabbit and her bunnies wander into Bevy's yard and nibble Mom's flowers and grapes that grow along the fence. Each time there is a new kindle of bunnies, Bevy tries to convince Mom and Dad to let her keep one as a pet since Old Charlie is too old to run and play with her.

Dad says, "Old Charlie has been a wonderful dog all these years and he's just fine just like he is." Old Charlie is a large shaggy dog that sleeps on the porch most of the time.

"Charlie's no fun, he doesn't even chase squirrels anymore," Bevy complained as she looked at old Charlie sleeping next to dad's chair.

"He lets the squirrels come up to take food right out of his bowl," she scowled.

"He's no fun at all, please can I have a new pet?" she asked sweetly.

Dad replied glancing over his newspaper, "Old Charlie has seen his better days. He's too old to be romping through the yard and rough housing with you kids. We'll discuss a new pet later Beverly Ann".

"Uh-oh, he only calls me Beverly Ann when he's serious, so I won't ask anymore right now," Bevy thought to herself.

After dinner, Dad sat up from his chair and reached for Bevy to hold her. He looked sad when he said, "You can't come with me to choir rehearsal tonight honey. Remember what the doctor said? It won't be much longer before you're completely up to snuff."

Dad scrubbed his stubby chin on Bevy's smooth cheek.

"Oh Dad, that tickles!" Bevy squealed and rubbed her scratchy cheek.

"It's okay, I'll play with my new friend, Puddin." Bevy ran upstairs to find Puddin Pie.

Puddin Pie is so shy, she won't let anyone else see her. She'll run and hide if anyone comes around. Whenever Bevy feels sad or lonely, Puddin Pie is always there to cheer her up. She has a loud, high-pitched voice with missing front teeth and the biggest smile you've ever seen.

She'll make you smile as soon as you see her walk into the room because it's about to be fun, total chaos and lots of laughing. She loves playing pranks on Grammy too, especially when Grammy is napping.

Grammy will usually just grunt and barely open one eye and say, "Is that you Bevy or that little bad friend of yours?"

The Great Revival

Every Sunday morning, Bevy's house smells like bacon and Mom's special muffins. You can hear Mom singing along with the radio while she buzzes around the kitchen with her hair in curlers.

Dad always makes sure the car is clean and shiny and all ready for church.

On this particular Sunday, Pastor Lacy announced "It's time for spring revival! Folks, it is the time for us to seriously seek

the Holy Spirit and be baptized in the name of Jesus Christ. The revival will commence on Wednesday night at 6:00 p.m. We will conclude with baptizing on Sunday morning. Amen? We will gather each evening outside under the big tent. Our youth choir will perform the opening night, and the visiting choirs will bless us with their heavenly voices on sequential evenings. Amen? We will also have dinner at church with our visitors, and everyone is expected to be on their best behavior, Amen!" Pastor said sternly as he looked over at Jacky, Cash, and the other boys seated in the back of the church. Cash sat up straight as if he had been paying attention the entire time.

The next week, Bevy's mom and the other ladies were all abuzz planning dinner menus for each night of revival.

After school, Bevy and her friends raced to the church for choir rehearsal. The girls also helped decorate the sanctuary and dining hall with fresh flowers for the big event.

The last day of revival ends on Sunday which is also baptismal day. Bevy has made up her mind to be baptized.

Bevy's excitement for revival had a different meaning for her than the other girls. This was her opportunity to get baptized and show everyone her commitment to Jesus Christ.

Her parents had not allowed her to be baptized before because they felt she was too young to make that decision.

Bevy argued with her parents that Pastor taught them all about baptism. He said, "baptism is a Christian practice that symbolizes a person's faith in Jesus Christ."

Bevy knew it was the right thing for her to do. She knew Jesus, and she believed His promise to her.

She wanted everyone to know she was serious about Him. He had in fact been with her at the hospital. She always talked with him, and she always remembered His promise to her.

Her parents finally realized her conviction was true and unwavering. So, they gave in and little Bevy was baptized during church revival just before Bevy turned eight years old.

Birthday Party

Springtime is also Bevy's birthday! Remember she's Daddy's June Bug!

This year Bevy is free from the hospital, and she is ready to spend time with her friends and classmates.

The party will be at Bevy's favorite tree.

The day of the party, Bevy looked like a princess in her pretty pink dress. Annette, Shirley, Barbara, and Mom wore pink outfits to match Bevy.

Grammy braided Bevy's hair which had grown past her shoulders since she had her big chop at the hospital.

As the party started, all the girls sat on one side of the tree enjoying cupcakes and punch. They whispered and made fun of the boys.

Of course, the boys were on the opposite side of the tree. When they weren't stuffing their faces with hotdogs and other snacks, the boys would race up and down the yard or wrestle each other, showing off for the girls.

Anthony Ellison was known as the class clown. All the girls thought he was kind of cute, but quite silly. He kept bouncing over to the girls table with a message from one of the boys.

"Yuck, go away," Barbara wrinkled her face and said in her soft shy voice.

"I think he's cute," Shirley spoke up in a flirty voice.

All the girls laughed at his silly antics, and he loved it!

The party was an enormous success. It ended with all the kids in the middle of the yard laughing and dancing together.

The next day Mom said, "Bevy you know it's time to go back to the doctor for more tests."

"Yep, I know, and I am not worried at all," she said as she skipped across the yard to her tree.

Mom and Dad appeared to be nervous about the new tests even though they pretended not to be. Grammy kept putting her hands on Bevy's head and whispering a prayer anytime she could reach Bevy.

Over the past weeks, Bevy noticed her parents' mood changing to nervousness. Bevy hadn't been feeling well, and she began to have problems with her appetite, and she was losing weight.

"I'm not sure what the big deal is. He promised me!" is all Bevy would say. She was calm and unbothered by the new tests.

However, she was looking forward to visiting with the kids at Children's Hospital. Of course, she always enjoyed seeing handsome Dr. Chari.

Bevy and Dad had been rehearsing **"He's Got the Whole World in His Hand"** with a different tempo and she wanted to perform it for the kids at the hospital.

The Final Tests

Finally, the morning came for the tests. Grammy prepared a big breakfast that morning, but Bevy couldn't eat very much.

She was excited about performing her song for the kids at the hospital.

Bevy and Mom went to the hospital appointment early and dad would meet them there later. The tests took all morning, and Bevy complained to her mom. "I'm ready to see the kids and sing my song." "Where is daddy?" she said impatiently.

"Just be patient sweety, we're going to meet Dad at the park. Your dad and I are going to meet with Dr. Chari after your test results are ready," Mom said softly.

The park is across the street from the Children's Hospital. It's filled with wonderful entertainment and music.

Some of the performers are doctors and nurses that enjoy performing and entertaining patients when they are not on duty.

Children's Park

Dad was standing at the ice cream truck studying the menu when Bevy and Mom walked over to him. He picked up Bevy and said, "Hey June Bug! What's your flavor today?"

The family enjoyed their ice cream while marveling at marionettes performing on the sidewalk. The puppets were amazing and so life like.

Bevy wanted to stay there and watch them perform, but Dad's phone buzzed. It was time to go back to Dr. Chari's office.

Test to Testimony

"He's Got the Whole World," Bevy had started singing before her parents and Dr. Chari could shut the door to the conference room. Mom and Dad giggled at each other.

After the meeting, Mom, Dad and Dr. Chari emerged from the conference room. For a moment they stood frozen and watched in amazement. Bevy was standing in the middle of the waiting room witnessing to little Clara, the parents, the nurses, and all the children about the love of Jesus Christ. She was sharing the story of her garden and the Lord's promise to her.

Tears were streaming down the cheeks of little Clara and the other parents in the waiting room as they witnessed this incredible child with her glorious testimony of hope and victory over disease and hopelessness. Her words were a message of hope to her parents, and to the other parents at the hospital.

Bevy's face was glowing, and her eyes were filled with jubilance as she spoke of the Love of Christ. She told them to have faith because healing is the Lord's Will for His children.

Bevy's parents and Dr. Chari stood there in astonishment and listened to the child speaking with such wisdom and boldness.

"The Bible says that whatever you ask for in prayer, you will receive, if you have faith. Always remember to ask the Lord to take care of your mommy and daddy and let them know that He is Lord and He is in control of everything. He is the Lord who heals, and He is the light for all the world to follow," Bevy proclaimed.

Little Bevy stood victoriously with her arms raised in worship as she wept and praised God. The room felt like it was covered in a warm blanket of love and peace.

It was then that Mom seems to find God's perfect peace. The peace that surpasses all understanding. She took a deep breath in and stood with confidence.

Mom dried her eyes, held her head up and said, "Amen and Amen".

Dad picked up Bevy, squeezed her tightly and said, "Yes baby you are right. The bible says, out of the mouth of babes and suckling, thou has perfected praise."

He put his other arm around mom and held them all together. He held them so tightly Bevy could hear his heart beating. Then from deep within Dad's chest, Bevy could hear a song rising and his beautiful voice began to sing, **"We Are the Heavenly Father's Children."**

Everyone stood right there in the middle of the waiting room listening to Dad's song and praising the Lord.

Another mother seated on the sofa softly whispered, "Hallelujah, Hallelujah" as tears streamed down her flushed face. She held onto her children tightly while she rocked back and forth to the rhythm of Daddy's song.

The nurse sat at her desk with her head bowed and her hands clasped in prayer posture.

For a while everything was still and quiet until Dad broke the silence by clearing his throat.

Then he stated, "There is nothing left to be said. There will be no worries to entertain. No matter what trials this family face from this moment on, we are going to live by the Promise of the **Almighty God!**

Bevy's Promise

Thank you for taking the time to read my book, and I sincerely hope you enjoyed Bevy's Promise.

Phyllis

Made in the USA
Columbia, SC
16 December 2024